FLYING SOLO

How RUTH ELDER Soared into America's Heart

JULIE CUMMINS
illustrated by MALENE R. LAUGESEN

ROARING BROOK PRESS
New York

RUTH ELDER didn't look at all like her name. At twenty-three years old, she was a beauty queen with a sparkling personality, a smile as bright as a toothpaste ad, and plenty of pluck.

She was fascinated with newspaper stories about Charles Lindbergh's solo flight across the Atlantic Ocean. After taking just a few flying lessons, she was determined to become the "female Lindbergh" and be the first woman to fly across the Atlantic.

It wouldn't be easy. In 1927, airplanes were a thrilling but dangerous novelty. Most people, men and women, believed that a woman belonged in the kitchen and not in a cockpit! Did that deter Ruth? Not one bit. She simply set out to prove them wrong!

On October 11, 1927, Ruth and her copilot, flying instructor George Haldeman, prepared to take off for Paris in *American Girl*, a plane as flamboyant as Ruth's personality.

Ruth posed on the wing of the plane with a picnic basket. She winked and blew a kiss to her fans in the press as she claimed she had two reasons for flying to France: she wanted to be the first woman to fly across the Atlantic Ocean and, "I have a desire to buy [a Parisian] evening gown and why not fly to Europe to buy it?"

Two-thirds of the way to their destination, after thirty-six hours in the air, an oil line on the plane ruptured—serious trouble. No land was in sight, but Ruth spotted a ship below them. With no radio contact or radar she grabbed two paper boxes, wrote *HELP* on them, and tossed them out of the plane. Luckily, one landed on the ship's deck. The captain pointed his ship toward land and quickly had a message painted on the deck that said the nearest land was 350 miles away—too far for the sputtering plane!

Ruth and George were forced to ditch *American Girl* in the water. Just minutes after they were rescued, the plane burst into flames.

Ruth declared, "We'll do it over again!" She never lost her courage or her lipstick.

When the ship reached Europe, Ruth had to *borrow* an evening gown. But she was instantly famous for her daredevil feat. The public had a new heroine. European royalty welcomed her; a tickertape parade was held in her honor in New York City. She was even invited to lunch at the White House

The New York Times

RUTH ELDER RESCUED · PLANE FALLS IN SE

FLAMES DESTROY
FLYING CRAFT AS
AVIATORS ESCAPE

Ruth signed a $250,000 vaudeville tour contract and Hollywood called! She appeared in two silent movies with western stars Hoot Gibson and Richard Dix. But even though she relished the spotlight, America's heartthrob wasn't ready to fold up her wings. She wanted to prove to America that she was a real aviatrix.

On August 18, 1929, Ruth and nineteen other women set out to show that women could fly airplanes just as well as men in the first women's cross-country air race. The pilots had more than headwinds to counteract. One reporter sputtered, "The only thing worse than dames in planes is dames racing planes!"

The day of the big event arrived with a buzz of excitement and anxiety. It would be no piece of cake. The zigzag route started in Santa Monica, California, and finished in Cleveland, Ohio, covering 2,759 miles. The racers would have to pilot halfway across the country using only roadmaps and their own two eyes to find their way.

Ruth, flying solo this time, wasn't the only attraction. Amelia Earhart, who had beaten Ruth by being the first woman to fly across the Atlantic Ocean, was favored to win this race, too. The other racers ran the gamut of experience, from aerobatic and transport pilots to plane builders, but they were all pioneers.

As the women strapped themselves in, checked their maps and emergency provisions—a gallon of water, milk tablets, and beef jerky—Ruth and several other women took a second to powder their noses. From then on, the race was called a powder puff derby.

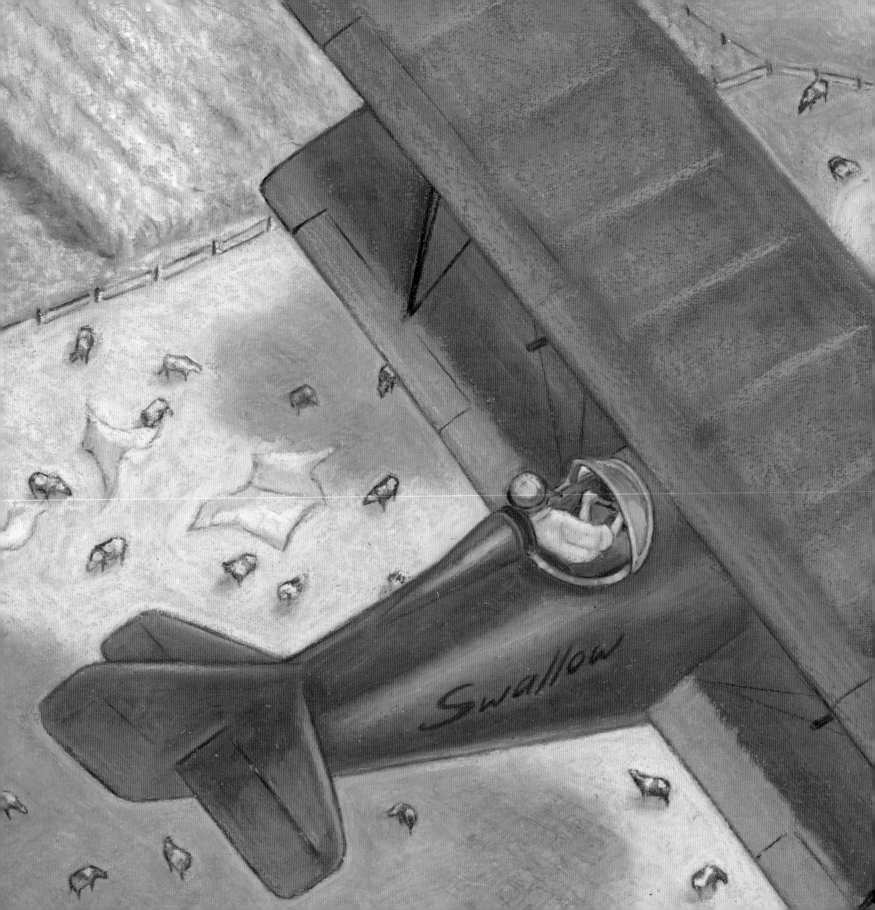

By nature, spunky Ruth wasn't easily cowed, but during the race she had a standoff with real cattle. On the second day, temperatures climbed to 120 degrees, causing extreme turbulence. The strong wind blew her maps over the side of the plane, and she landed in a farmer's field to get her bearings and fill her water bottle. As luck would have it, cattle were grazing in the pasture and all Ruth could think about was her plane— her red plane! "Please God, let them [all] be cows!" she prayed.

But the farmer's wife was a bigger threat. Washing clothes outside in a washtub, she marched over to the plane and yelled at Ruth for scaring the cattle. Ruth didn't dillydally; she just swung the plane around and took off! The story became the favorite and most embellished tale of the Derby.

At every stop on the racecourse, crowds gathered to cheer the women on. On the last leg, a farmer in Ohio plowed a huge arrow in the middle of his harvested corn crop, pointing toward Cleveland. The female pilots dipped their wings to him in appreciation.

Ruth got lost a few more times, but she never lost her determination to prove she was a competent flyer and she could finish the race. It took nine days of grit and gumption, but Ruth finished the course, placing fifth. She stood proudly beside the winner, Louise Thaden, and the other women pilots who had shaped aviation history. They had proven that women could fly as well as men.

Ruth didn't leave it there. She adamantly claimed that American women would be fighter pilots in the future.

And she was right.

AUTHOR'S NOTE

It's hard to imagine a time when American women didn't have the choices or freedom that we do today. Yet Ruth Elder's hop, skip, and skyward leap from beauty pageants to flying airplanes was not just daring but outright shocking. When the first transcontinental women's air race took place on August 18, 1929, women were continuing to strive for equal rights, having only won the right to vote in 1920.

Nevertheless, glamorous Ruth charmed the press and public. Even her hairstyle set a fashion trend as *Vogue* magazine featured a photo of her wearing her "Ruth Ribbons," the colorful scarves that she used to tie her hair.

At the time of the Powder Puff Derby, there were only seventy-five US-licensed women pilots and only forty of them met the race requirements of having one hundred hours of solo flight. Will Rogers, a nationally known humorist and pilot himself, was the announcer and chief cheerleader. Just before the start gun, when he saw several women pull out compacts to powder their noses, he said, "It looks like a Powder Puff Derby to me!" The name stuck and is still used today.

In the 1920s and 1930s the role of women was changing. Previously closed windows were beginning to open as women exercised their freedom outside of the home. Ruth and her fellow pilots were at the forefront of this movement. Even so, women pilots still had hurdles ahead.

Ruth's statement that American women would become fighter pilots did come true, but it took decades. In World War II women pilots were hired and trained to ferry aircraft from factories to military bases. Called WASPs, Women's Airforce Service Pilots, they were employed by the government to fly in noncombat conditions. Because the women were hired as civilian pilots, neither they nor their families received any military pay or benefits. It took over fifty years for these dedicated women to receive the recognition they were due. On July 1, 2009, they were presented with the Congressional Gold Medal.

Ruth Elder died in 1977 at the age of seventy-four.

SOURCES AND FURTHER READING

BOOKS: Blair, Margaret Whitman. *The Roaring 20: The First Cross-Country Air Race for Women*, National Geographic, 2006.

de la Croix, Robert. *They Flew The Atlantic*, Frederick Muller, 1958.

Homan, Lynn M. and Thomas Reilly, *Women Who Fly*, Pelican, 2004.

Jessen, Gene Nora. *The Powder Puff Derby of 1929: The True Story of the First Women's Cross-Country Air Race*, Sourcebooks, 2002.

Lomax, Judy. *Women of the Air*, Dodd, Mead, 1987

Moolman, Valerie. *Women Aloft*, Time-Life Books, 1981.

MAGAZINES AND NEWSPAPERS: *Aero Digest*, "The American Girl," November, 1927.

Journal Herald, obituary, October 11, 1977.

Los Angeles Times, obituary, October 11, 1977.

WEB SITES: www.women-in-aviation.com

www.aerofiles.com/powderpuff.html

www.ninety-nines.org

DVD: *Breaking Through The Clouds: The First Women's National Air Derby*, written and directed by Heather Taylor, Archetypal Images, 2010.

A KEY TO THE FLYERS ON THE FINAL PAGES

1. Gladys O'Donnell **2.** Opal Kunz **3.** Ruth Elder **4.** Louise Thaden **5.** Amelia Earhart **6.** Blanche Noyes

1. Harriet Quimby: first American woman to hold a pilot's license (1911). **2. Ruth Elder 3 and 6. Ann Baumgartner:** WASP, flew test planes during WWII. **4. Betty Turner:** Women in Airforce Service Pilot (WASP) **5. Amelia Earhart:** first woman to fly solo across the Atlantic Ocean **7. Kara Hultgreen:** first female naval carrier-based fighter pilot **8. Dawn Dunlop:** fighter pilot, commander of 412th Test Wing, Air Force Flight Test Center, Edwards Air Force Base. **9. Sharon Preszler:** first female active-duty fighter pilot. **10. Marie T. Rossi:** first woman to serve as an aviation commander during combat. **11. Shawna R. Kimbrell:** first black female fighter pilot. **12. Nicole Malachowski:** first female pilot to be part of the USAF air demonstration squadron, the Thunderbirds. **13 and 14. Martha McSally:** first female commander of a USAF fighter squadron. **15. Eileen Collins:** first female commander of a space shuttle; carried Louise Thaden's flying helmet into space.

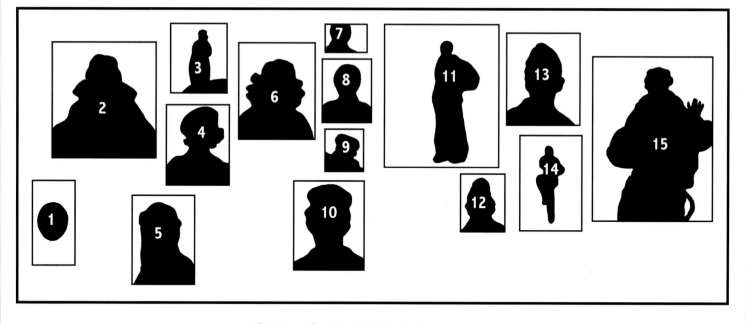

"[FLIGHT] IS A SPIRIT TOTALLY FREE.
FLIGHT IS YESTERDAY'S YEARNING.
THE FULFILLMENT OF TODAY'S DREAMS.
TOMORROW'S PROMISES."
—LOUISE THADEN